Our Solar System:

THE SUN

by Gary Rushworth

Table of Contents

Pictures To Think About

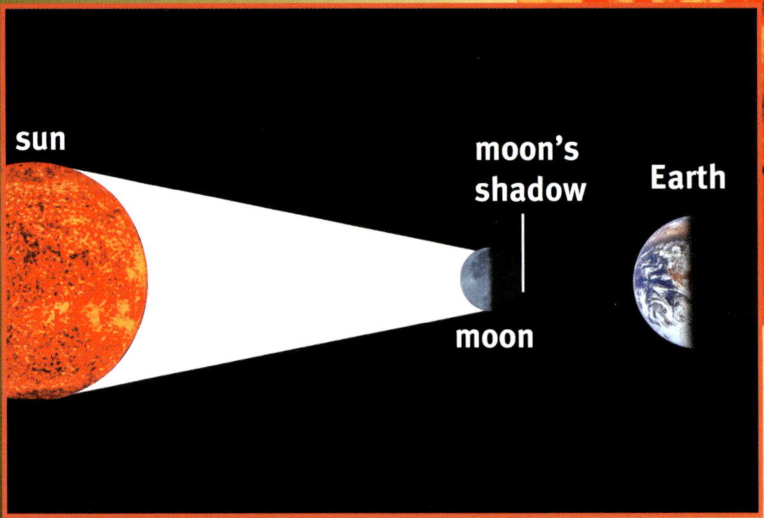

Our Solar System: The Sun

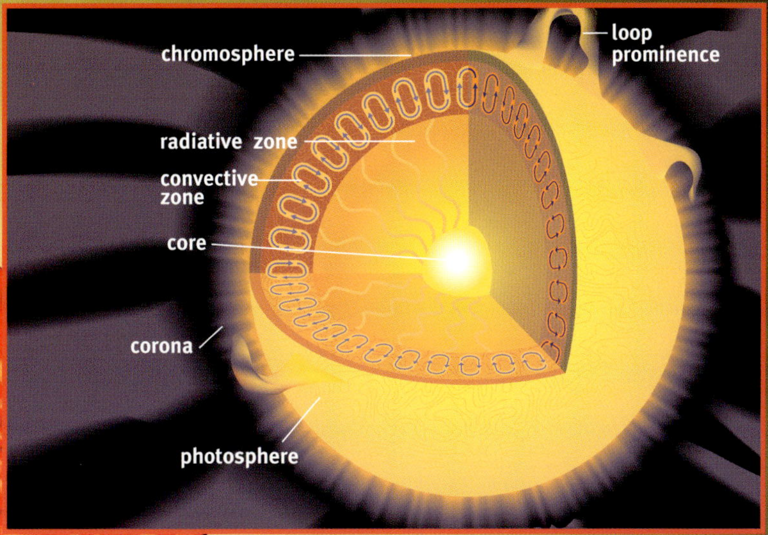

Words To Think About

Characteristics

- moon blocks the sun
- happens every year
- ?

eclipse

What do you think the word **eclipse** means?

Examples

- annular eclipse
- total eclipse
- ?

heliocentric

What do you think the word **heliocentric** means?

Greek: ***helios*** **(sun)**

Greek: ***kentrikos*** **(center)**

Read for More Clues
eclipse, page 16
heliocentric, page 5
orbit, page 5

orbit

What do you think the word **orbit** means?

- What things **orbit** the sun?
  - Mars
  - ?
  - Earth
- What happens as Earth **orbits** the sun?
  - Earth travels
  - ?
  - seasons change

Introduction

The sun is important. Plants need the sun. Animals need the sun. People need the sun, too. The sun makes life on Earth possible.

The sun gives us light. The sun gives us energy. The sun warms the air around us. It warms the water, too. It affects the weather.

The sun helps us track time. Earth moves around the sun. This movement gives us four seasons.

In this book, you will read about the sun. You will learn what the sun is. You will see how the sun shapes our lives.

It's a Fact

The sun is 4.6 billion years old!

The Sun and Our Solar System

What is the sun? The sun is a star. The sun is more than one million times larger than Earth. The sun is not a very big star, though. It is only a medium-sized star. The sun looks big to us because it is the closest star to Earth.

▲ The sun is much bigger than Earth.

Math Matters

The sun is the biggest star we can see using just our eyes, but there are more than one billion stars in the universe. The next closest star is more than two million times farther away. Look at this diagram of the sun next to one of the biggest stars scientists have discovered. You can see how small our sun is in comparison.

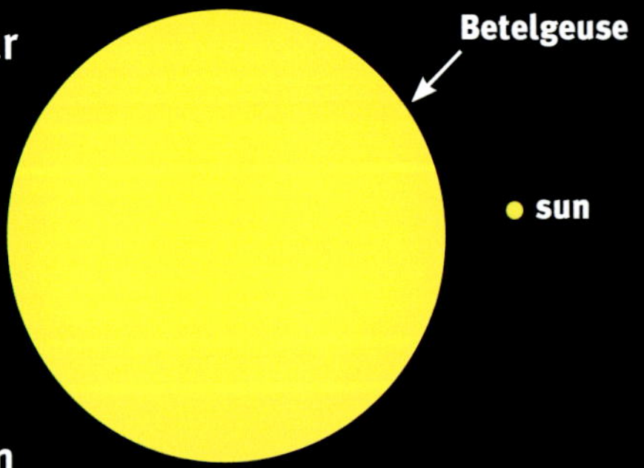

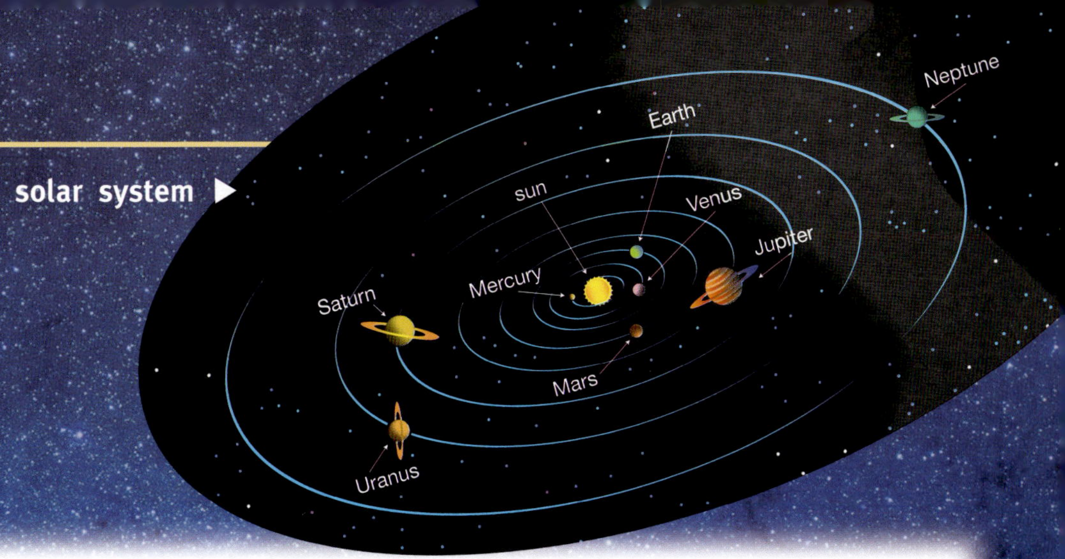

Our solar system is **heliocentric** (hee-lee-oh-SEN-trik). This means the sun is the center of our solar system. Our solar system has one sun and eight planets. Our solar system has moons, asteroids, and comets. It also has dwarf planets.

The planets **orbit** (OR-bit), or travel around, the sun. The sun's gravity pulls on the planets. The sun's gravity holds the planets in place.

Historical Perspective

In ancient times, many people thought of the sun as a god. The early Egyptians named the sun Ra. The Aztec believed the sun was a god in charge of heaven. Apollo was the god of the sun for both the Greeks and the Romans. We know today that the sun is a star.

The Sun and Our Seasons

Why does Earth have seasons? Different parts of Earth get different amounts of sunlight. This happens partly because Earth is round.

Earth's North and South poles receive the least sunlight. The **equator** (ih-KWAY-ter) gets the most sunlight. The equator is an imaginary line around Earth. The equator divides the planet into two parts. The parts are called hemispheres (HEH-mih-sfeerz). The top part is the Northern Hemisphere. The bottom part is the Southern Hemisphere.

Because Earth is round, and its axis is tilted, sunlight strikes some parts of the planet more directly than others. ▼

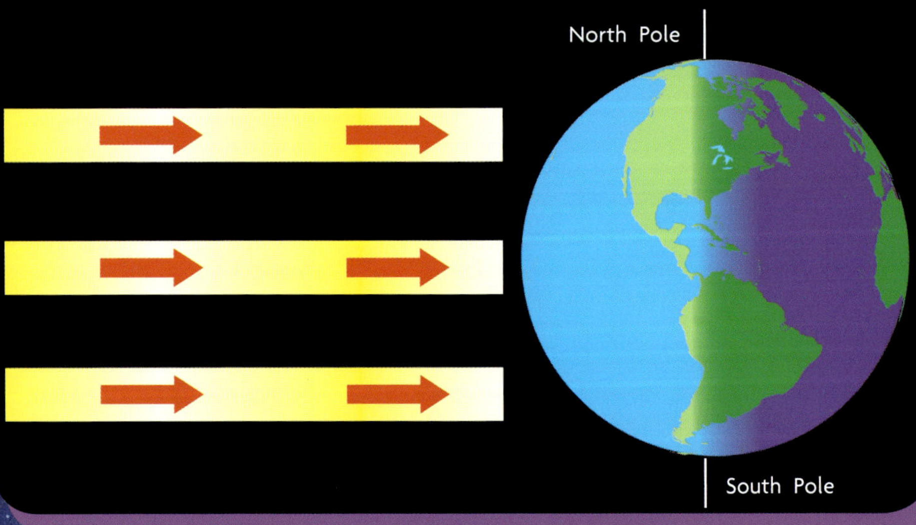

Everyday Science

How long does it take for Earth to travel all the way around the sun? It takes about 365 days, or one year.

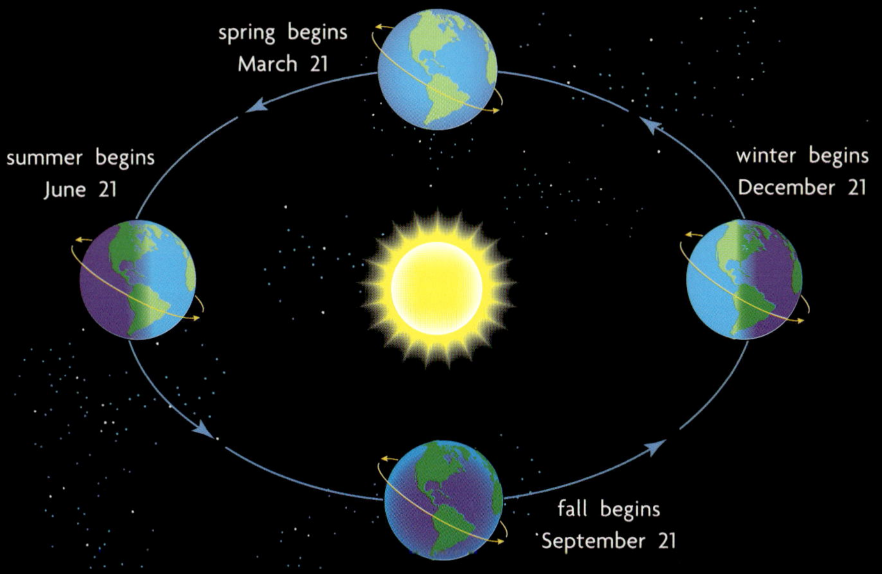

Earth rotates, or spins, as it orbits the sun. When the Northern Hemisphere faces the sun, it is summer in the northern half of the planet. When the Southern Hemisphere faces the sun, it is summer there. Places around the world have different seasons at the same time. When it is winter in North America, it is summer in Australia!

They Made a Difference

Claudius Ptolemy (TAH-leh-mee) and Nicolaus Copernicus (koh-PER-nih-kus) were scientists. These two men studied the sky. They changed the way people think about the universe.

Ptolemy was a great astronomer and mathematician. He was born in A.D. 85. He wrote many books about the stars and planets. His ideas are still famous today.

Ptolemy thought that Earth was the center of the solar system. He thought that the sun and planets revolved around Earth. His theory (THEER-ee), or idea, is known as the geocentric (jee-oh-SEN-trik) theory. Geo means "Earth." Centric means "center."

People believed Ptolemy's thoughts for the next 1,400 years. Here is what he said about his love of astronomy and the stars:

"Well do I know that I am mortal, a creature of one day. But if my mind follows the winding paths of the stars, then my feet no longer rest on earth . . ."

◀ Claudius Ptolemy

Copernicus was born in 1473. He was born in Poland. Poland is a country in Europe. Copernicus worked in medicine. He studied astronomy in his free time.

In 1513, Copernicus wrote a book. The book was about the heavens. Many years later, he wrote another book. The book was called *On the Revolutions of the Heavenly Spheres*.

Copernicus said that the planets revolved around the sun. The word *centric* means "center." *Helio* means "sun." His theory was called the heliocentric theory. Most people did not believe Copernicus. Then, in the 1600s, scientists Galileo (ga-lih-LAY-oh) and Isaac Newton proved him right.

Copernicus was given a copy of his book on his deathbed. In the book he wrote:

"Finally we shall place the sun of himself at the center of the Universe."

Nicolaus Copernicus ▶

The Mass of Gas

Can you live on the sun? The answer is no. The sun is very hot. The sun's surface, or outer layer, is about 11,000 degrees Fahrenheit (6,100 degrees Celsius). Water boils at 212°F (100°C). The sun's surface is more than fifty times hotter than boiling water. Ouch!

What is the sun made of? The sun is a ball of hot, exploding gases. Most of the sun is made up of the gas **hydrogen** (HY-druh-jen). The rest of the sun is made up of the gas **helium** (HEE-lee-um).

▲ the sun's surface

Tiny bits of hydrogen join together to make helium. This process gives off heat and light. This heat and light is what we feel and see on Earth.

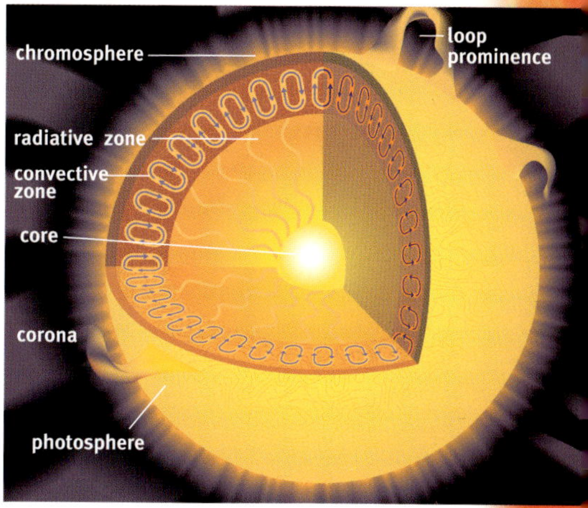

Inside the Sun

The surface of the sun is very hot. Still, the surface is the coolest part of the sun.

The sun is made up of layers. The **core** (KOR), or center, of the sun is the hottest part. The core can be 27 million °F (15 million °C). The sun's energy is created at the core. The energy then travels up to the surface.

The next layer is the **radiative zone** (RAY-dee-ay-tiv ZONE). Heat from the core moves through this zone in waves. The **convective zone** (kun-VEK-tiv ZONE) is next. This layer is made of gas currents. The currents carry the sun's energy to the surface.

Everyday Science

To match the energy produced by the sun, you would have to set off 100 billion tons of dynamite every second.

The Sun's Surface

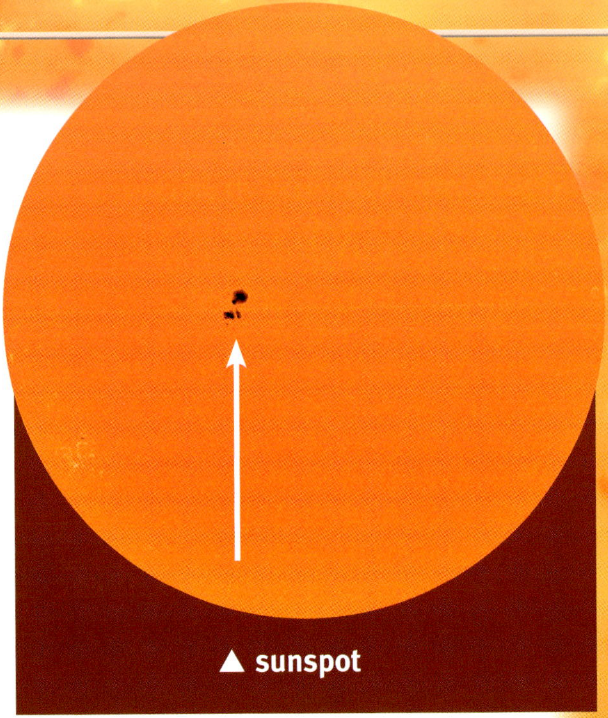

The surface of the sun is called the **photosphere** (FOH-tuh-sfeer). This layer is where the energy from the core bursts out in a blaze of light. Most of the light that we see comes from the photosphere. Above this layer is the chromosphere.

The sun has dark spots on its surface. We call these spots **sunspots**. Sunspots appear darker than the rest of the sun's surface because they are cooler. They can be any shape or size. Some sunspots stay for a few hours. Others stay for weeks. The sun's magnetic fields cause sunspots.

It's a Fact

The word *photosphere* comes from Greek terms meaning "ball" and "light."

Solar Wind, Solar Storms

Did you know that there is wind on the sun? **Solar wind** (SOH-ler WIND) is not like wind on Earth. The sun always gives off bits of energy. You cannot see the energy, but it is there. This energy is solar wind.

▲ solar wind

The sun has storms. The sun's storms are different from storms on Earth. The sun's storms are magnetic storms.

Some magnetic storms look like giant loops or arches. These storms are **solar prominences** (SOH-ler PRAH-mih-nents-es). The loops curve away from the sun's surface.

Solar flares (SOH-ler FLAIRZ) are sudden explosions. Solar flares release magnetic energy. Strong solar flares can affect radio signals on Earth.

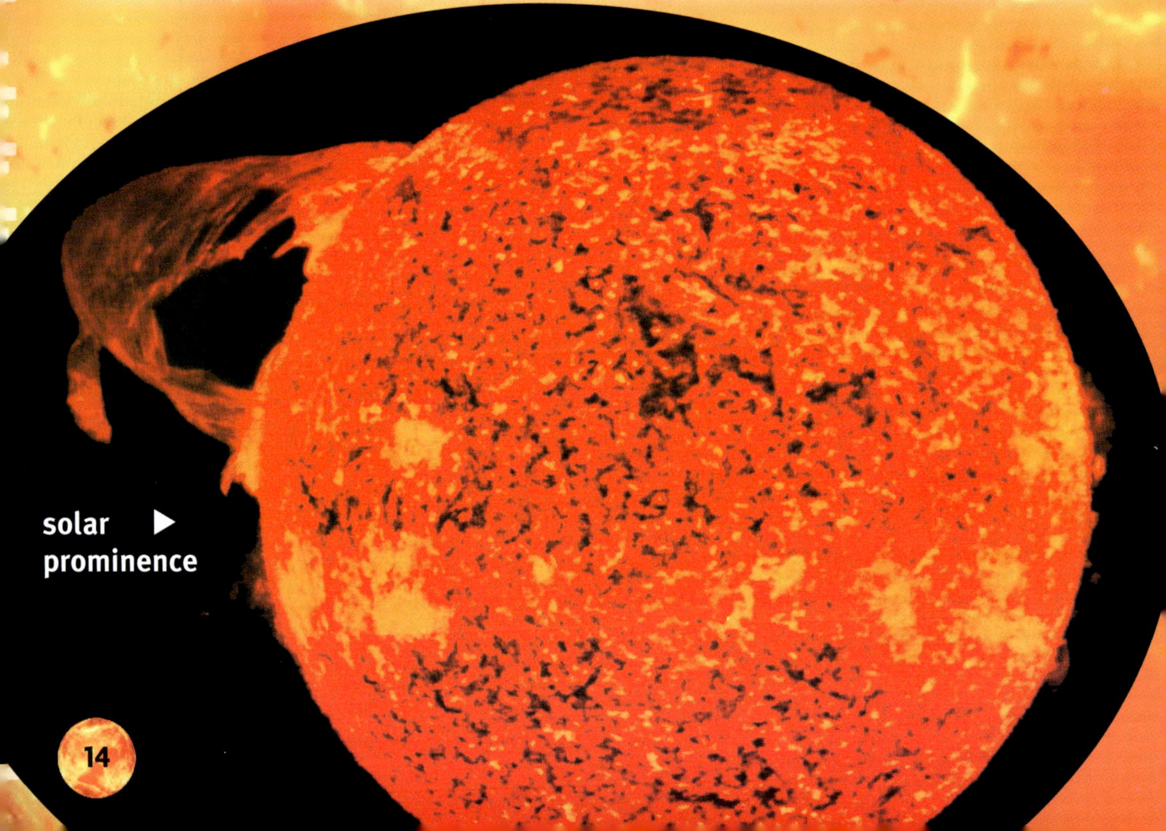

▲ the Northern Lights

Aurora Borealis

Earth's core is like a giant magnet. On the surface of Earth, the magnetic pull is strongest at the North and South poles.

Sometimes particles of solar wind become trapped near Earth's poles. When this happens, the solar particles crash into the air in Earth's atmosphere. This crash makes the atmosphere glow and we see a solar light show in the sky.

This display of lights and colors is called the aurora borealis (uh-ROR-uh bor-ee-A-lis), or Northern Lights. The Northern Lights happen in Earth's Northern Hemisphere. A similar light show happens in the Southern Hemisphere. This display is called the aurora australis.

Solar Eclipses

Solar **eclipses** (ih-KLIPS-ez) happen when the moon passes between the sun and Earth. For a short time, the moon blocks all or part of the sun's light. Between two and five solar eclipses happen every year.

Long ago, people were afraid of solar eclipses. People did not understand why eclipses happened. People feared the sun might not come back. Many people told myths to explain eclipses. In China, people said that a dragon tried to eat the sun. People would make loud noises. They thought noise would scare the dragon and bring back the sun.

These girls are watching an ▼ eclipse that happened on March 29, 2006.

solar eclipse ▶

Today, scientists can tell when an eclipse will happen. They know years in advance.

Different Kinds of Eclipses

The sky does not always turn dark during an eclipse. The sky only turns dark during a total eclipse. A total eclipse is when the moon completely hides the sun. Only the **corona** (kuh-ROH-nuh) can be seen. The corona is the outermost part of the sun's atmosphere.

A total eclipse can be seen from only some places on Earth. In 2006, people in Brazil saw a total eclipse. People in parts of Africa and Asia could also see the eclipse.

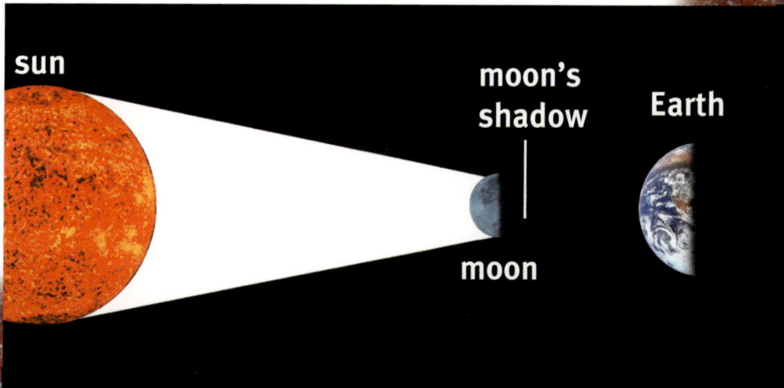

▲ a total eclipse

An annular (AN-yuh-ler) eclipse happens when the sun and the moon are exactly in line. The sun looks like a small ring around the moon. This type of eclipse can last twelve minutes.

A partial (PAR-shul) eclipse is when the sun and moon are not exactly in line. The moon blocks only part of the sun. This type of eclipse can be seen from many places on Earth.

✔ Point

Visualize

Imagine what it would be like to experience an eclipse without understanding the science behind it. With a partner, act out how you would feel and what you would say.

It's a Fact

Right before and after an eclipse, you can often see a big ray of sun peeking out from behind the moon. This is known as the diamond ring effect.

Total Solar Eclipses 2001–2015

Date	Maximum Duration	Where Visible
March 29, 2006	4 minutes, 7 seconds	Atlantic, Northern Africa, Central Asia
August 1, 2008	2 minutes, 27 seconds	Greenland, Arctic, Russia, China
July 22, 2009	6 minutes, 39 seconds	India, China, Pacific
January 15, 2010	11 minutes, 8 seconds	Africa, East Europe, Asia, the Middle East
July 11, 2010	5 minutes, 20 seconds	Southern Pacific Ocean
January 4, 2011	5 minutes, 40 seconds	Europe, Arabian peninsula, North Africa, Western Asia
July 11, 2015	5 minutes, 20 seconds	South Pacific

◀ March 29, 2006

Conclusion

We still have a lot to learn about the sun. Scientists send many spacecraft out to collect data about the sun.

In 1990, the *Ulysses* (yuh-LIH-seez) spacecraft was launched. This spacecraft orbits over the sun's poles. It studies solar wind.

▲ the *Ulysses* spacecraft

The *SOHO* spacecraft was launched in 1995. *SOHO* orbits the sun. It flies about 1,000,000 miles from Earth. That is about four times as far as the moon. *SOHO* can give us our first long-term view of the sun. *SOHO* will help us understand how the sun affects life on Earth.

▲ *SOHO*

TRACE was launched in 1998. *TRACE* lets scientists study the magnetic fields on the sun.

✔ Point

Read More About It

What questions do you still have about the sun? Ask your teacher or librarian to help you find books and Internet sites where you can search for answers.

The sun is the center of our solar system. It makes life on Earth possible. The weather, seasons, and time depend on the sun.

The sun has been around for over four billion years. Scientists say that the sun will shine for five billion more years. That is good news for us all!

▲ The sun will keep shining down on Earth for many years to come.

Glossary

convective zone (kun-VEK-tiv ZONE) a region of the sun where the energy from the core travels on currents of hot gas (page 11)

core (KOR) the central part of the sun (page 11)

corona (kuh-ROH-nuh) the outermost part of the atmosphere of a star (page 17)

eclipse (ih-KLIPS) the total or partial hiding of a planet, star, or moon by another (page 16)

equator (ih-KWAY-ter) an imaginary circle around the center of Earth (page 6)

heliocentric (hee-lee-oh-SEN-trik) sun-centered (page 5)

helium (HEE-lee-um) a light, colorless element that is found in various natural gases (page 10)

hydrogen (HY-druh-jen) a colorless, odorless gas (page 10)

orbit (OR-bit) the path traveled by one body in space around another (page 5)

photosphere (FOH-tuh-sfeer) the shining surface of the sun or a star (page 12)

radiative zone (RAY-dee-ay-tiv ZONE) a region of the sun where energy leaves the core (page 11)

solar flare (SOH-ler FLAIR) a sudden outburst of particles and energy from the sun's surface (page 14)

solar prominence (SOH-ler PRAH-mih-nents) a mass of gas hanging in the sun's atmosphere (page 14)

solar wind (SOH-ler WIND) the continuous radiation of charged particles from the sun's surface (page 13)

sunspot (SUN-spaht) one of the dark spots that appear from time to time on the sun's surface and are usually visible only through a telescope (page 12)

Index